YOUR KNOWLEDGE HAS VALUE

AF145452

- We will publish your bachelor's and master's thesis, essays and papers

- Your own eBook and book - sold worldwide in all relevant shops

- Earn money with each sale

Upload your text at www.GRIN.com and publish for free

Bibliographic information published by the German National Library:

The German National Library lists this publication in the National Bibliography; detailed bibliographic data are available on the Internet at http://dnb.dnb.de .

Imprint:

Copyright © 2019 GRIN Verlag
Print and binding: Books on Demand GmbH, Norderstedt Germany
ISBN: 9783668976023

This book at GRIN:

https://www.grin.com/document/489008

Giuliana Scotto

The Use of Force in International Law

On the Historical Evolution and Actual Content of the Prohibition

GRIN Verlag

GRIN - Your knowledge has value

Since its foundation in 1998, GRIN has specialized in publishing academic texts by students, college teachers and other academics as e-book and printed book. The website www.grin.com is an ideal platform for presenting term papers, final papers, scientific essays, dissertations and specialist books.

Visit us on the internet:

http://www.grin.com/

http://www.facebook.com/grincom

http://www.twitter.com/grin_com

Prohibition of the Use of Force in International Law.

Historical evolution and current content of the prohibition.

(Excerpt from G. Scotto, *Diritto internazionale per filosofi*, II. ed. riveduta e ampliata, Grin, München 2014, pp. 167-207, translated into English by the author with few updating data and modifications)

Table of contents

1. Introduction. The most important rule in international law

Both the common sense and many scholars with historical or political background – therefore without expertise in international law – approach international law with the prejudice that war, whose presence is witnessed throughout the history as an element which cannot be eliminated from human affairs, would be a tool which States can still and always legitimately use. War and more generally the possibility of resorting to armed force would represent the counter-proof of the thesis which considers the international society as an example of the state of nature, of the war condition of all against all: the hobbesian condition of *homo homini lupus* («*every man is a wolf for any other man*»).

Despite the fact that history records many cases of resort to armed force in international relations – that is, in the community of those entities characterized by the principle of sovereign equality – the consideration of States' practice in international law does not allow to conclude that in general the use of armed force in international relation is permitted. Quite on the contrary, an adequate analysis of the current international order demonstrates armed force is prohibited as a principle, with the sole exception of self-defence, and that recently such a prohibition has assumed peremptory character. Because of the devastating effects which, at the time of atomic and mass destruction weapons, the use of armed force could produce on the possibility itself of the coexistence of the international subjects, the prohibition of the use of force has become the most important rule in international law and its respect is one of the most important factors which guarantee the coexistence of States and ultimately the very survival of the human race.

2. Notes on the historical evolution of the prohibition of the use of armed force

Even scholars willing to extend the hypotheses of exception to the prohibition of the use of armed force currently in force[1] cannot disregard that since its arising from the dissolution of the *Respublica of Christian peoples*, international law has increasingly provided for limitations of the use of arms[2]. First of all, the practice of aggression has always been considered illegal, unless it was justified for sanctioning purposes. Since the dawning of international law, a distinction has been established between «just war» (*bellum iustum*), admitted as a reaction to an illegal act, and «unjust war» (*bellum iniustum*)[3], considered in itself illegal. For Grotius, in substance, «just war» means execution of the law, that is, an instrument for reacting to a wrong suffered, and in general it can be used only when it is strictly necessary[4]. Considering that the text of Grotius dates back to 1625 and by tracing the official birth of international law back to 1648, it is as if international law since ever provided the prohibition of the use of force at least for aggressive purposes; it is as if the limitation of the use of force was inherent in international law. With the birth of the international society, peaceful coexistence was immediately considered not as a mere «absence of armed conflict» (as a secondary effect of a social contract which has somehow put an end to a more original and authentic conflict dimension), but as a «condition which characterizes the normality of international relations»[5], with respect to which, in this initial historical phase, war is both a breach of peace (as «unjust war») and an instrument of peace (as «just war»).

Furthermore, it must be stressed that, since the dawning of international law, war can be unjust not only when it constitutes the implementation of an unjustified aggressive policy towards another international subject, but also when it takes the concrete form of a disproportionate measure. The requirement of proportionality

---

[1] For instance W. Michael Reisman, «Present Problems of the Use of Force in International Law, B. Sub-group on Humanitarian Intervention», report presented to the *Institut de Droit International*, Santiago Session 2007, Pedone, Paris 2007, pp. 171–201, at 200 f.
[2] See Benedetto Conforti, *Comment on Reisman, Institut de Droit International*, Santiago Session 2007, Pedone, Paris 2007, pp. 201-207.
[3] Hugo Grotius, *De jure belli ac pacis. Libri tres* (1625), Officina Wetsteniana, Amsterdam reprint 1712, Liber I, Caput I, § III, p. 3.
[4] Hugo Grotius, *De jure belli ac pacis*, Liber II, Caput XXIV, § IX, p. 615
[5] Giorgio Badiali *Il diritto di pace di Alberico Gentili*, Il Sirente, Fagnano Alto 2010, p. 6.

characterises immediately the rules on the possibility of using the armed force: even if the use of force is justified as a sanction, it ceases to be lawful whenever it exceeds the proportion with respect to the offense suffered. The requirement of proportionality is thus harboured at the root of the possibilities of resorting to armed force: the need to fit the sanction to the unlawful act is affirmed at the origin of international law as the *raison d'être* of the set of legal rules which guarantee the coexistence between international subjects, that is to say those concerning international responsibility – probably the most delicate area of the entire international order. «Proportion», *«raison d'être»*, that is *«rational»*, *«ratio»* of the norm: it is no coincidence that these features of the most important legal rule of international law are all possible translations of the Greek word **lógoj** (logos) in which they are gathered together. Reflecting on the historical origin of the limits to the use of armed force, we grasp more deeply the intimate connection between **lógoj** and law.

From the preceding considerations, the common feeling that in international law, at least as a «just» measure, war is a lawful – or at least a permitted – instrument, could at first sight find some support; but a deeper consideration of the contemporary international rules on the matter allows to conclude that not only the notion of just war is no longer admitted in international law, but also that the possibility to resort to force is in principle banned from the international legal order. If for a relatively long lapse of time (until the middle of the nineteenth century) the notion of just war, in the above-mentioned sense, is not even put in doubt in the relations between States, the improvement of the war instruments (in particular the availability of long-range weapons) gives rise to the need to further limit not only the *jus ad bellum* (i.e. the legitimate possibility of resorting to armed force, that is to say the just war), but also the *jus in bello*, that is the concrete possibilities of the right to use weapons (which kind of weapons and against whom) once the conflict has broken out. Starting from the last decades of the nineteenth century, States begin to conclude a series of increasingly numerous agreements aimed, for example, at excluding the use of armed force against the civilian population, the wounded, and prisoners of war: we can think to the Geneva Convention of August 22, 1864 for the Amelioration of the Condition of the Wounded in Armies in the Field, later replaced by the Geneva Convention of July 6, 1906 for the Amelioration of the Condition of the Wounded and Sick in Armies in the Field; the Petersburg Declaration of 1868 Renouncing the Use, in Time of War, of Explosive Projectiles Under 400 Grammes Weight; the II Hague Convention of 29 July 1899 regarding the Laws and Customs of War on Land.

As in the second decade of the twentieth century, the first great conflict had as a consequence that blood was shed all over the world, at its conclusion States realize the opportunity to limit in itself the recourse to war, i.e. also to the «just» war (although, as we will see, without prejudice to the right of legitimate defence, that is the right to resort to armed force in order to repel an armed attack). From this point of view, at the end of the First World War, the Treaty of Versailles of 1919 establishing the League of Nations represents an epochal turning point. It is the first time that States create an international organization focused on the commitment of the Member States to refrain themselves from the use of armed force and to take into account what a common body will establish in this regard. According to Article 10 of the Covenant of the League of Nations,

«[the] The Members of the League undertake to respect and preserve as against external aggression the territorial integrity and existing political independence of all Members of the League. In case of any such aggression or in case of any threat or danger of such aggression the Council shall advise upon the means by which this obligation shall be fulfilled».

However, although the League is highly innovative in its scope, it is marked by a structural weakness constituted by the fact that the right to resort to the just war (i.e. the war for sanctioning purposes) undergoes in practice only a procedural limitation. In this regard, Article. 12 of the Covenant of the League of Nations establishes that

«[the] Members of the League agree that if there should arise between them any dispute likely to lead to a rupture, they will submit the matter either to arbitration or to inquiry by the Council, and they agree in no case to resort to war until three months after the award by the arbitrators or the report by the Council».

The Covenant of the League of Nations, therefore, does not in itself prohibit resort to war as a method of settlement of international disputes, but only sets a time limit of three months in order to induce the State intending to wage war to ponder adequately on its intention. Furthermore, it should be noted that the notion of «war» is an international legal concept which embraces the situation which takes place following a specific declaration, while other, for instance less serious modalities of resorting to armed force not preceded by a war declaration, cannot be interpreted as «war» (for example armed reprisals and some self-defence operations on the borderline between the state of necessity and self-defence), remaining, therefore, as a kind of measure, fully legitimate even under the terms of the Covenant. In short, the Covenant does not limit the use of armed force for sanctioning purposes, but only the war as declared war; furthermore the limit does not encounter war itself, as a measure considered under a substantial point of view, but only places a temporal condition (the lapse of three months from the judicial decision or arbitration authority or the report of the Council of the League of Nations) to make use of it.

A further step forward in the evolution of the matter, is represented by the Pact of Paris of 27 August 1928, also known as the Briand-Kellogg Pact (due to the names of the French and US representatives participating in the negotiation as plenipotentiaries). The Pact of Paris represents a progress with respect to the Covenant of the League of Nations, because it prohibits war *tout court* as a means of resolving disputes and as an instrument of international policy. In this regard, Article 1 of the Pact of Paris states:

«[t]he High Contracting Parties solemnly declare in the names of their respective peoples that they condemn recourse to war for the solution of international controversies, and renounce it, as an instrument of national policy in their relations with one another».

But even in this case we have a twofold weakness. On the one hand, only the resort to war, and not to every kind of use of armed force, is prohibited (therefore armed reprisals remain lawful, as indeed attested by the practice of those years; as well as all those methods of resorting to armed force not falling within the notion of war); on the other hand, no sanctioning mechanism alternative to the war is established, particularly no restriction in the use of armed force is provided for in the case of violation of the prohibition to refrain from resorting to war. Despite the fact that, within 1939, 63 States had adhered to the Pact of Paris, the convulsive thirties of the twentieth century testify the fragility of this system and quickly ruined towards the second great world conflict. If we did not go beyond the first months of 1945, the harshness of the Second World War and the very serious violations of human rights perpetrated on that occasion would perhaps authorize us to conclude that conflict really represents the deepest essence of human relations without residues and that any attempt to limit this evil, wild, aggressive feature that marks us indelibly is vain.

It is so much more surprising than in the spring of 1945, in San Francisco, just as the Second World War with all its tragedies was coming to an end, something completely opposite to that feature is devised, namely the creation of an international organization which is not only founded on respect for international law in general, but also finally enshrines effectively the prohibition of using armed force. Article 2§4 of the Charter of the United Nations, thus, represents the cornerstone of the evolution of the matter, and at the same time the greatest effort to overcome the previous failures: not the acceptance of our familiarity with war and destruction, but the most serious attempt, if not of their elimination at least of their containment through the clear, very broad statement of the prohibition of the use of force in the following terms:

«[a]ll Members shall refrain in their international relations from the threat or use of force against the territorial integrity or political independence of any state, or in any other manner inconsistent with the Purposes of the United Nations».

As can be seen from the text of Article 2§4 just mentioned, not only the actual use of force is prohibited, but also its threat; and the concept of prohibited force is intended in a very wide sense, since not only «armed» force is forbidden but «force» *tout court*.

But before asking whether the term «force» in Article 2§4 embraces other form of measures than the armed ones, we can first remain on the question of *armed* force, undoubtedly. Through Article 2§4 an attempt was made to formulate the prohibition of use of armed force in the broadest and most complete manner, thus trying to repair the defects of the previous agreements: thanks to Article 2§4 of the Charter any kind of armed measure – other than self-defence, as we will see – adopted unilaterally is now prohibited and *prima facie* it amounts to an internationally wrongful act. In fact, Article 2§4 is not limited to the possibility to wage war, but the prohibited force is intended in a the widest sense. It means, for instance, that in the framework of the UN Charter, armed reprisals – typical international unilateral sanctions, which could be conceived as a sort of «just war» seen before – are no longer admitted. On the other hand, the banning of the possibility to resort to armed force unilaterally, is balanced by the creation of an alternative mechanism operating in a concerted manner which, thanks to its sophisticated decision-making process, should protect against the abusive use of weapons: namely the collective security system, whose heart is represented by the Security Council. In other words, if until the first half of the twentieth century, States could use armed force for both defence and sanction purposes, the Organization of United Nations operates a sort of a split with respect to the exercise of this faculty: the mechanism of collective security, on the one hand, subtracts from the individual States the faculty of resorting to force (except for self-defence), and, on the other hand, treasuring the experience that it is perhaps not realistic in an anarchist community, like the international society, even to hope to completely annul the faculty of unilateral recourse to the armed force, by establishing the centralization of the management of crises of a certain gravity under the Security Council which, due to its composition and the operation conditioned by the veto power of the five permanent members (United States, Soviet Union, Great Britain, France, China), such a system should ensure special prudence in the decision on the possible use of armed force. The centralization of crises on a body composed of several States should not only remove the abuses that are always present in a unilateral evaluation of the situation, but would correspond in some ways to the desire to make the international society – interpreted by many as «primitive», as it is grounded on self-defence mechanisms – evolve towards that process of centralization which characterizes the evolution of the State, conceived, according to a vision of Hegelian memory, as the most complete institution to which human life caught in its relational aspect could ever hope for.

The system outlined in San Francisco provided that the Member States should make available to the Security Council armies and military means in ways that would be determined in *ad hoc* agreements (Article 43 of the Charter). Such armed forces should constitute the United Nations army under the command of a Military Staff Committee formed by the Chiefs of Staff of the five permanent members and directed by the same Security Council. The removal from the States of the faculty of unilaterally resorting to armed force was therefore counterbalanced by the provision of this collective security system equipped with its own armed forces. Now, as known, such a military mechanism has never been implemented. Not only the *ad hoc* agreements which should place military assets at the disposal of the Security Council have never been stipulated, but also for a long time the decision-making mechanism of the vetoes has almost paralyzed the activity of the Security Council itself. Nevertheless, this failure of the collective security system was not followed by the revival, for the individual States, of the full faculty to use the armed force as envisaged by international law in the period prior to the Second World War. Not without surprise – if we consider that the international society does not have authoritative mechanisms –, the States have not claimed, as perhaps one would have expected, the restoration of the power to use armed force, but have even pushed the prohibition referred to in Article 2§4 beyond the contractual limits of the United Nations system and have not hesitated to make it – firstly – a general, customary rule, therefore binding also for the non-member States, and – then, quickly, within a few decades – even a peremptory rule.

The prohibition to resort to force has therefore consolidated as the most important norm of current international law and the only exception allowed is self-defence. Of course, with this assumption, we do not want to disregard the number of occasions in which, over more than half a century of the life of the United Nations, the prohibition has been violated. As we will see later, the issue of the limits to the use of armed force has received new attention when, with the end of the Cold War, the Security Council began to function – often in a manner that does not comply with the Charter; and especially after the attack on the Twin Towers in 2001, part of the doctrine sought to enlarge the scope of the possible exceptions to the prohibition of the use of armed force in order to have more effective means in the fight against international terrorism.

However, these attempts to enlarge the scope of the only exception to the prohibition of the use of armed force, in other words the attempts to widen the limits of admissibility of self-defence, have proved to be not only unconvincing, for they have been criticized by the States, but also, from a logical point of view, they do nothing but confirm the full validity and cogency of the prohibition in question. As noted by the International Court of Justice in the case *Military and paramilitary activities in and against Nicaragua* (§186), precisely with regard to the rules prohibiting the use of force, «[i]t is not to be expected that in the practice of States the application of the rules in question should have been perfect, in the sense that States should have refrained, with complete consistency, from the use of force or from intervention in each other's internal affairs. The Court does not consider that, for a rule to be established as customary, the corresponding practice must be in absolutely rigorous conformity with the rule. In order to deduce the existence of customary rules, the Court deems it sufficient that the conduct of States should, in general, be consistent with such rules, and that instances of State conduct inconsistent with a given rule should generally have been treated as breaches of that rule, not as indications of the recognition of a new rule. If a State acts in a way prima facie incompatible with a recognized rule, but defends its conduct by appealing to exceptions or justifications contained within the rule itself, then whether or not the State's conduct is in fact justifiable on that basis, the significance of that attitude is to confirm rather than to weaken the rule».

As can be seen from this clear reasoning, the presence of elements of the practice contrary to the prohibition of the use of armed force are not configured in such a way as to seriously cast doubt on the fact that this rule is still *fully* in force in international law and indeed constitutes the norm most important among those that compose the same *jus cogens*.

To confirm what we have seen so far, we can think only of the very recent affair involving Russia and Ukraine[6]. On the one hand, some Western powers (the United States and the European Union) considered the behaviour of Russia to amount to an act of aggression, but with regard to this they expressed the firm intention of resorting only to economic measures (to confirm of the fact that armed measures are banned by international law). For its part, probably with the purpose to minimize its responsibility in the affair, Russia has affirmed (in a manner not far from being a pretext) that the Russian troops penetrated into Ukraine would have acted on voluntary basis and not as organs of the Russian State, thus declining the own responsibility for the act of aggression and at the same time confirming the full validity of the prohibition of the use of armed force in international law.

3. Nature of the prohibited force. Armed force and economic coercion

Since the Security Council began to «function», from 1990 onward, the debate on the use of force has interpreted the term «force» essentially as meaning «armed force». Nevertheless it must be recalled that, some years before the fall of the Berlin wall, some scholars, considering the serious economic crisis that occurred during the seventies, had opened the question whether the forbidden force should be limited only to the use of arms, or extended to coercive measures of different nature, for example political or economic force, at least when it took the form of measures of considerable gravity[7]. This broadening of the notion of forbidden force had found the support by the developing countries and indeed, given the growing interdependence between States, as a consequence, it allows to consider as in substance analogous to an act of armed aggression the situation suffered by a State which, depending economically in everything and for everything from another, is forced by the latter through economic measures to behaviours which it would never adopt in a different situation. An economic

---

[6] Especially in the developments up to the end of August 2014, on which see Maurizio Arcari «La crisi in Crimea», in *Diritti umani e Diritto internazionale*, vol. 8, n. 2, 2014, pp. 473-479.

[7] See for instance Richard B. Lillich, «Economic Coercion and the International Legal Order», in *International Affairs*, vol. 51, No. 3, 1975, pp. 358–371.

strangulation could essentially materialize a violation of the sovereignty of the State or of its political independence. This orientation, moreover, lost importance when, with the end of the Cold War, the practice of the Security Council brought to the fore the issue of armed force and the limits of its use. Nevertheless, in the contemporary society tending towards total globalization from an economic point of view, it is perhaps not unlikely to expect within a short time a resumption of this attempt to extend the notion of forbidden force even to economic measures of a significant gravity, in order to protect more effectively the sovereignty and independence of States. More recently, in the context of the United Nations, the question has arisen whether the economic measures decided by the Security Council must not infringe a minimum level for the survival of the civilian population and whether they may result in a violation of the economic position of States to which the measures adopted are not direct. Someone[8] argues that, following the entry into force of the Charter in the UN, such questions would have given rise to the consolidation of a customary norm limiting the resort to economic measures. Actually, it seems to me that, in the terms in which the question seems to have been posed so far, it is an application of the general limits of the «principles of humanity» which, already before the entry into force of the Charter, were envisaged for the adoption of reprisals. Although measures of the UN Security Council are not properly «sanctions», this limitation of the principles of humanity seems to have been grafted onto international law since long time, since the first attempts to regulate the *jus in bello*. Another issue is whether, in general, the use of prohibited force should be understood in an broad sense, also including economic coercion to the extent that it can be considered as equivalent to armed force, which should lead to consider as illegal even retortions (that is unfriendly retaliatory acts, not amounting to a violation of international law) of a considerable gravity (for example, the refusal to enter into a commercial treaty − what a State would always be free to do − with a State whose economy totally depends on the exchanges which could be carried out thanks to the treaty to stipulate).

---

[8] Benedetto Conforti, Carlo Focarelli, *Le Nazioni Unite*, IX ed., Cedam, Padova 2012, p. 267.

4. The exceptions to the prohibition of the use of armed force: the collective security system

Once it is clarified that both the threat and the use of armed force are prohibited in international law, it is necessary to dwell on the exceptions admitted to this prohibition. In this regard, a first distinction must be drawn according to whether the permitted armed force materializes in a measure adopted by a State unilaterally, or it is a measure adopted by the Security Council in the exercise of its responsibility for maintaining and restoring international peace and security. Given that the system envisaged by the Charter is based on this sort of counterbalance, that is to say, the attempt to centralize the use of force through the security system is sourced from the subtraction from the States of the general faculty of threatening or using armed force. collective, I will first outline this system briefly.

The maintenance of international peace and security is the primary responsibility of the Security Council (Article 24 of the Charter). Although many provisions concerning the Council are spread in various parts of the United Nations Charter (on the other hand, the Council is the most important body of the UN, firstly because its decisions are mandatory for Member States), it can be affirmed that the duties of the Council with regard to the maintenance of international peace and security are essentially gathered in two fundamental Chapters of the Charter, Chapter VI and Chapter VII.

Chapter VI (including Articles 33 to 38) is dedicated to the peaceful settlement of disputes. Examining the provisions of this Chapter, it is clear that in matters of dispute settlement the Security Council can only address recommendations to States, that is non-binding resolutions. The prerequisite for the adoption of such recommendations is that there is a controversy or a situation of a certain gravity: in order for the Council to be able to take action based on Chapter VI the dispute or the situation must be such that its continuation is «likely to endanger the maintenance of international peace and security» (Article 33 of the Charter). In such a case the Council can play a mediating role, that is, it can invite the States parties of the dispute to adopt the so-called peaceful means for dispute settlement; or, pursuant to art. 37§2, it can indicate «terms of settlement», that is it can suggest the parties a solution on the merits. So briefly: on its own initiative, the

Council can consider a dispute between States: 1) only if the dispute presents certain traits of gravity; 2) and adopting only recommendations (regarding the procedure or the merits), but never imposing a binding decision on the States involved. Only if the parties expressly request it, the Council may make recommendations regarding a dispute regardless of its seriousness (Article 38 of the Charter), but even in this case it cannot adopt mandatory resolutions (i.e. decisions).

Therefore, as regards the solution of international disputes or situations of a certain gravity as indicated in Article 33 mentioned above, the Council can only adopt recommendations and not decisions, i.e. it cannot impose a solution on the merits according to which the dispute should be composed, nor indicate in a compulsory manner for the parties which means of settlement they shall resort to. At the most, the Council can remind the parties that legal disputes must be referred to the International Court of Justice, or it can confirm their obligation of peaceful settlement in force under Article 2§3 of the Charter by inviting the parties to adopt such means. The clarity of the Charter on the nature of the Council's competences in the field of settlement of disputes and/or situations is not surprising: the Council is a political body and has neither the time of reflection, nor the skills, nor the specialist knowledge, not even the experience and the impartiality of a judge. Its function is that of a policeman who tries to avoid the aggravation of a certain dispute or situation which could lead to an escalation dangerous for the entire planet. I insist on this point because, instead, during the nineties we had an overlapping of functions of the Council (between Chapter VI and Chapter VII) in this matter.

But we shall proceed step by step.

If under Chapter VI the Council can only adopt recommendations, its powers are much more significant pursuant to Chapter VII, dedicated to action to protect (= to maintain and/or restore) peace and in which the Council can address States compulsory decisions.

Chapter VII opens with Article 39, according to which: «[t]he Security Council shall determine the existence of any threat to the peace, breach of the peace, or act of aggression and shall make recommendations, or decide what measures shall be taken in accordance with Articles 41 and 42, to maintain or restore international peace and security». So, firstly, Article 39 of the Charter indicates the conditions legitimating the action of the Council: but threat to peace, breach of the peace or act of aggression are three hypotheses which the Charter does not define further, but which are intended as more serious in comparison with those envisaged in Chapter VI. Regardless – for the moment – of how these three conditions shall be interpreted, the occurrence of one of them, pursuant to the same Article 39, allows the Council to recommend and/or decide peaceful measures (exemplified in Article 41) and/or measures involving the use of armed force (exemplified in Article 42).

With regard to the definition of threat to peace, the breach of the peace or the act of aggression, the Council itself ascertains their existence as legitimate prerequisites for its action, but it does not mean that the Council may declare the existence of one of such prerequisites if they actually do not occur. As already observed, although the Charter does not define such prerequisites of the action for the action of the Council, these three prerequisites imply the existence of a situation whose gravity justifies the action of the Council. In order to define the nature of such situations in accordance to the Charter, for the case of aggression, the Council can find some help by referring to General Assembly Resolution 3314 (XXIX) on the Definition of aggression (see the text in the Appendix) adopted in 1974 precisely in order to facilitate the concrete determination of cases in which the aggression is far to be evident and unmistakable. In the other two hypotheses the Council indeed does not avail itself of a similar instrument of interpretation; however, if we look at the practice of the Council, it should be noted, first of all, that it tends to avoid – for political reasons – to refer to «aggression» in its resolutions. On the verge of very serious armed attacks – as it was when Iraq attacked Kuwait in 1990, where the aggressive nature of the Iraqi act was out of question – it preferred to speak of «breach of peace», and in general the notion of «breach of the peace» tends to be used for very serious hypotheses of disturbance to international peace and security. «Breach of the peace» is referred therefore to very serious situations in which armed force is used and which could even be interpreted properly as acts of aggression.

But what should be understood under the concept of «threat to peace»? Compared with the «breach of the peace», from the name it sounds to be a much more nuanced hypothesis, where a situation of open conflict has not yet burst out. It shall be recalled here that the Council has the main responsibility for the maintenance of *international* peace and security. It would imply that the nature of the «threat to the peace» shall be relevant at international level, i.e. be of such gravity as to threat the peaceful relations among the States and other subjects of the international community, and not, for instance, by itself, involve questions threatening national, internal peace. One would think of internal conflicts which, because of their gravity, could extend over the national borders, or could give rise to armed reactions on the part of other international subjects. Although the name «threat to the peace» leaves room to the possibility to extend this notion to situations in which the use of armed force is absent or only latent, it should nevertheless be noted that in the practice of the organ prior to the fall of the Berlin wall – a practice nevertheless made by few resolutions: about 600 resolutions from 1945 to 1989 – as «threat to peace» nevertheless understood situations of international conflict or internal conflict but of such gravity as to be able to assume the characteristics of the international conflict overflowing from national borders. Instead, after the end of the Cold War, the notion of threat to peace has been extended to situations not properly characterized by the use of weapons, where on the contrary the possibility of the use of weapons (properly the «threat», that is the looming grave danger of the use of armed force) was not even in question. In these cases, it seems that the Council has inaugurated an *extra vires* practice, not in accordance with the letter of the Charter. The diminishing of power by the Soviet Union after the end of the Cold War has in fact initiated a practice in which the notion of «threat to peace» has even been abused. In the *Lockerbie affair* in particular (see SC Resolutions 731 and 748 of 1992), the Security Council declared the existence of a threat to peace consisting in Libya's refusal to extradite the alleged perpetrators of two attacks to two civilian aircraft (the first occurred in Lockerbie in Scotland in 1988, and the second occurred in Nigerian airspace in 1989) whose victims were mainly US, French and British citizens. Although the whole case amounted to a dispute in the sense of Chapter VI mentioned above (where the Council can only

17

adopt recommendations), in the *Lockerbie affair*, following Libyan obstinacy, the Security Council, managed in greatest freedom by the three western superpowers, declaring the existence of a threat to the peace, decided some economic measures against Libya in order to force the latter to extradite the alleged terrorists. Libya, on its part, started a proceeding before the International Court of Justice. But the Court – very pavidly, in my opinion – preferred to decline its competence as regards the question to indicate the content and the limits of the Security Council's power to «determine the existence» of the prerequisites referred to in Article 39 of the UN Charter, and in particular the content of the «threat to the peace», thus paving the way to those views, mostly shared in the subsequent years by some not very forward-looking scholars, which considered the Security Council as being essentially *«legibus solutus»* when determining the condition to action according to Chapter VII of the Charter. Such conjuncture, arisen after the end of the Cold War, actually gave rise to nothing but vague principles, in fact depending on the features of a certain concrete political situation. In this way, on the one hand, it is not possible to identify certain, clear rules which help to evaluate beyond doubts such recent practice of the Council; and, on the other hand, it is not possible to foresee with sufficient reliability the nature of the situation in which an action by the Security Council is to be expected, thus divesting the Council itself of its own authority.

In the light of these considerations, further resolutions can be read as not based on the letter of the Charter. Among these, SC Resolution 687 (1991) stands out, with which, at the end of the Gulf War, the Council essentially imposed war damages on Iraq, periodic inspections to verify the possible illegal possession of prohibited weapons, as well as the definition of the borders with the Kuwait; but also Resolution 1546 (2004) with which the Council has in fact covered with a semblance of «international» legitimacy the establishment of an interim Iraqi government (supported by the approval of the United States), providing it with the tools for its material strengthening (by the creation and training of one of its armies by the multinational local force, including US and British military personnel; by drafting a constitutional charter with the help of the UN Secretary-General, providing economic means by means of the establishment of a special development fund etc.) regardless of the principle of self-determination of the local population. Further instances will be examined later.

Faced with these examples of the practice clearly overriding the limits of the Charter, part of the doctrine[9] has drawn the conclusion that not only in determining the existence of a threat to peace, but also in ascertaining violation of peace and an act of aggression the Council would be entirely *legibus solutus* and its assessment would be unquestionable. Now, this part of the doctrine, which perversely accepts whatever the Council decides, relies essentially on the lack of a legal *ex-post* control on the Council's assessment. But reflecting on the structure of international law, analyzing the preparatory works of the Charter and, above all, noting – what characterizes the phenomenon of the international organization in general – the widespread, great reluctance of States to renounce consistent slices of competences and powers and attribute them to collective organs, it is quite unlikely that UN Member States intended and nowadays intend to confer such a vast power on the Security Council, in practice to decide, without any limit, when to adopt, against an international subject, measures which could even be unjust or illegitimate. Therefore, in particular those doctrinal positions according to which the threat to peace would be a fluid concept, creating a sort of blank delegation for the Council, leaving it in practice free to decide whatever measures seem appropriate, sound really inadequate. In other words, the «threat to peace» laid down in Article 39 as one of the preconditions enabling the Council to act, cannot be a mere formal qualification, that is, an empty concept –separated from a content identifying a specific concrete situation –, capable of covering any situation in which the contingent arrangement among the States voting in the Council deems appropriate to act using the tools of Chapter VII. For the word to correspond to the thing – an essential requirement in legal hermeneutics, and not only – «threat to peace» must necessarily be a grave situation, in which a serious danger is hanging over international peace: just as this notion had been more consistently interpreted during the Cold War, when its

---

[9] See for example Benedetto Conforti, Carlo Focarelli, *Le Nazioni Unite*, IX ed., Cedam, Padova 2012, p. 236.

interpretation corresponded to a widely shared mode of understanding this kind of assumption.

Nor, in my opinion, could it be said that «by now» the Security Council has broadened its powers «in fact» or «in practice», that is, by developing a «customary» rule modifying the Charter, thus extending the scope of the hypotheses in which the Council can act under Chapter VII. The evaluation of many situations in which the Council invokes the existence of a threat to peace in order to act under Chapter VII, is not based on the widespread consent of the international community nor is free from criticism. In one of the most recent cases, SC Resolution 1973 (2011) with which the Council qualified the situation of civil war created in Libya as a threat to peace, did not find full support even from the few States voting in the Council: in fact, it was adopted with the favourable vote of only ten members, while five (all very important and influential States, both from an economic and a political point of view: China, Germany, India, Brazil and Russia) abstained, expressing rather their own concern for the situation and the desire to find a peaceful solution for it.

Therefore, bearing in mind these problems linked to the existence of the conditions for action on the basis of Chapter VII, which in my opinion do not amount to formal notions, but can only interpreted in an effective, actual sense, corresponding to the facts of reality, it is now necessary to consider more deeply what the Council can do once the existence of a threat to peace, a violation of peace or an act of aggression is declared.

The Council can adopt basically three kinds of measures, laid down in three different Articles of the Charter: provisional measures (Article 40), measures not involving the use of armed force (such as the suspension or blocking of economic traffic, of communications, diplomatic relations: see the non-exhaustive list thereof under Article 41) and measures involving the use of armed force (military actions with air, naval or land forces: see Article 42). While there is no doubt that the measures referred to in Articles 41 and 42 can be both recommended and decided by the Council, the question is less clear as regards the measures referred to in Article 40, because their content is not specified: Article 40 simply establishes that the Council can invite the parties to adopt the measures which appear «necessary or desirable». In the practice, invitations to the parties involved to cease fire or to withdraw their troops from a certain territory are usually interpreted as provisional measures; but the alternative formulation between «necessary» measures and «desirable» measures has given rise to doubt about the binding nature of these measures as such[10]. Consistent with the approach followed so far, and not limited to the question of the binding nature of provisional measures, it does not seem that the Council is likely to impose on States – even on a provisional basis – «what it wants» (what *appears* to him as «necessary»), in the sense of a boundless will which leads to arbitrariness. Even the sovereign quality of the States as subjects of international law cannot be understood as arbitrariness and it is far-fetched to conclude that the Security Council has been given a capricious, arbitrary decision-making capacity, which not even the subjects of international law themselves possess. States, on their own, are not endowed with a will intended as a capricious faculty and therefore could not confer on the Council such faculty (or competence) which they themselves do not possess. A confirmation that this is the key to interpret the question of the binding nature of provisional measures, comes from Article 40 itself, where it is established that in any case provisional measures cannot prejudice the rights, claims and positions of the parties concerned. Thus, the Council can indeed remind the parties to comply with rights and duties already existing upon them on the basis of other norms of international law: for example, the withdrawal of troops (because there is a rule which prohibits the military invasion of the territory of another international entity), cease fire (because in international law the use of force is not allowed), opening of negotiations or adopt other means of peaceful settlement (because international disputes must be settled pacifically). But the Council could not impose terms of regulation or new rights and obligations with prejudice of the parties involved.

On the contrary, as regards the measures not involving the use of armed force (Article 41) and those involving the use of armed force (Article 42), in these cases and in accordance with the letter of the Charter, the Council can either decide in a compulsory

---

[10] Hans Kelsen, *The Law of the United Nations. A Critical Analysis of Its Fundamental Problems*, Frederick A. Praeger, Inc., New York 1950, p. 739 ff.

manner for States or only recommend such measures. In general, if the measures are intended to be binding, the Council adopts the verb «to decide» («[t]he Security Council decides ...», sometimes also indicating Article 41, more often making a generic reference to Chapter VII of the Charter); while in the case of only recommended measures it uses the verb «to call upon» («[t]he Security Council calls upon...»), implying the only exhortative effect of the action of the Council.

As already mentioned, the list of peaceful and military measures pursuant to Articles 41 and 42 is not exhaustive. But beyond the fact that other types of measures could be devised in addition to those expressly listed, it is however necessary to distinguish these two types of measures by the nature they can assume in the light of Article 2§7 of the Charter of the United Nations, according to which «[n] Nothing contained in the present Charter shall authorize the United Nations to intervene in matters which are essentially within the domestic jurisdiction of any state or shall require the Members to submit such matters to settlement under the present Charter; but this principle shall not prejudice the application of enforcement measures under Chapter VII». In the light of the most consistent doctrine on the subject[11], this provision shows how deeply the Charter of the United Nations is based on the principle of the sovereign equality of the Member States, which, in other words, means that the Organization does not has a supranational nature, it cannot interfere in the reserved domain (so-called domestic jurisdiction) of the States, i.e. within the relations (of an eminently inter-individual nature) which the State manages as a sovereign entity, therefore through the exercise of its legislative, executive and judicial powers. But Article 2§7 provides that this impossibility for the United Nations Organization to «intervene» into sovereignty, that is into the internal affairs of a State, suffers an exception, namely the case of the coercive measures referred to in Chapter VII of the Charter. What shall be intended as «coercive measures»? The aforementioned best doctrine on this point, in consistency with the approach proposed, intends, with this expression, that coercive measures are the military measures referred to in Chapter VII, therefore, so far as we have seen, those foreseen in

---

[11] See Gaetano Arangio-Ruiz, «Le domaine réservé. L'organisation internationale et le rapport entre droit international et droit interne», Cours général de droit international public», *Recueil des Cours de l'Académie de Droit International de la Haye*, tome 225, 1990-IV.

Article 42, but not those of Article 41[12]. Leaving aside for the moment the question of the subject endowed with the task to adopt such military measures (whether the member States of the United Nations or the Chief of Staff of the permanent members of the Security Council), in the light of the Article 2§7 just mentioned the distinction on the nature of the measures runs along the line of discrimination which isolates the «coercive» (i.e. armed) from the non-coercive, a class comprehending both provisional measures pursuant to Article 40, as well as peaceful measures pursuant to Article 41. Why should armed measures violate the reserved domain? According to the most consistent view mentioned a few lines above, this kind of measures is able to violate the domestic jurisdiction due to the fact that it consists materially in intrusive acts of territorial sovereignty: for example the invasion of the territory of a State by armies, or the capture of individuals, the removal of buildings or infrastructures. Such measures are capable of violating the domestic jurisdiction – i.e., the internal sovereignty of the State – because their adoption takes the form of acts replacing State power, directly affecting the level of the inter-individual relations dominated by the State as subject of international law. If, for example, such armed measures consist in the capture of individuals, they are placed on the same level (they have the same material effect) of the capture of individuals ordered by the legitimate police forces within the State. The military force carrying out the action pursuant to Article 42 has a power analogous to that of the legitimate force of domestic law. However, this similarity is limited to a factual feature: the State addressed by the military measure *de facto* suffers an interference in its own internal affairs, but cannot be *legally* forced, from the point of view of its own internal right, to give a normative continuity, to integrate into a single continuous juridical system the legitimacy of military measures under Article 42 with those that it would adopt in the exercise of its own sovereign powers. In other words, the legal decision originating from the Security Council and with which the military intrusive measure of the internal affairs of a State is

---

[12] See Gaetano Arangio-Ruiz, «Le domaine réservé», *op. cit.*, p. 141. Different from this approach is the position of Kelsen, *The Law of the United Nations*, op. cit., p. 744, who instead extends the coercive nature to the measures referred to in Article 41, coherently with the assumption from which he starts, that such measures of the Security Council, although not involving the use of force, would have the nature of sanctions. On this point see *infra*.

carried out is, juridically speaking, external with respect to the internal legal order of that State, it is a pure fact: this means that, in case of contrast of the Security Council decision with other national provisions, internal legal subjects are *legally* bound to respect these latter provisions and *not* the Security Council decision. In other words, between the international legal order, or, in this case, the legal order of the United Nations, from the one side, and the national legal order on the other side, there is a discontinuity, a gap, a duality: it is the consequence of the fact the sovereign nature of the State as a subject of international law.

But if, from a factual point of view, measures involving armed force under Article 42 can infringe *de facto* the domestic jurisdiction of the State, thus resembling to internal coercive measures adopted by the police or army forces, the measures referred to in Article 40 and in Article 41 of the Charter are far from possessing such similar nature. When the Council decides this type of measures (in line with the provisions of Article 25 of the Charter), it addresses States indicating which behaviours they must adopt and *these* behaviours are mandatory: for example, the Security Council decides that against a certain State an economic embargo must be adopted with the exclusion of pharmaceuticals and basic necessities to safeguard the principles of humanity for the benefit of the civilian population (as happened against Iraq with SC Resolution 661 of 1990). But it is in the jurisdiction of the States to decide, at their internal level, how, i.d. with which legal means, to implement these economic measures in practice, to establish which types of goods should be considered essential, which companies are in any case entitled to export products to the State affected by the embargo and which ones should interrupt their traffic; which pharmaceutical products should be exempted from the embargo and which not. And if a State, in implementing the obligation to adopt the embargo as decided by the security Council, makes a mistake in this assessment, or deliberately fails to comply with the obligation to carry out the embargo, or, because of a serious internal institutional crisis, is not able to adopt the measures in accordance with the decision of the Council, the latter cannot substitute itself to the organs of the State and adopt in its place the internal norms for the concrete implementation of the embargo. It cannot do so because it does not have the possibility of adopting internal

24

acts in substitution of the powers of the State, because the State is sovereign and its internal juridical operators would not observe similar Council commands as they are subject to the power of the State – which, as such, has the power, the tools to compel, both *de facto* and legally, individuals to do what the State has established, while on the contrary the Security Council has no power in this regard.

We can take another example: the well-known affair of the two fusiliers of the Italian navy held in New Delhi awaiting trial. Undoubtedly, the prolongation of the situation of imprisonment of the two individuals without a regular imputation violates one of the fundamental human rights, that of the reasonable duration of the trial. Regardless of Italy's responsibilities – many aspects still need to be clarified in this regard –, there is no doubt that India, in this affair, is violating a fundamental norm of international human rights law. Well, even if the situation in the future should transcend and evolve into a threat to peace, thus legitimizing the Council to deal with the issue according to Chapter VII of the Charter, the peaceful measures that the Council could decide could never legitimately take the form of a release order in substitution of an order with the same content which Indian judicial authorities could have adopted. An impossibility of this kind derives from the fact that the Security Council is not superordinate to the State of India, and therefore it does not have authoritative powers on the judicial organs of the latter. On the contrary, if an Indian judge of domestic law, legitimately invested with the matter, should order the release of the two Italian soldiers as an exercise of his or her internal power, the soldiers would be released as a *legal* result of the execution of the order of that judge.

In reality, the measures not involving the use of the armed force that the Council can adopt cannot *per se* (they do not have the power to) violate the domestic jurisdiction of a State, and this because the UN is not a supranational organization.

* * * * * * *

25

A final consideration concerns the nature of the measures referred to in Chapter VII of the Charter. Both the media language and some authors use to qualify such measures as «sanctions». But on closer inspection, even from the rapid excursus just described, it is clear that the Security Council is not endowed with sanctioning functions.

First of all, the prerequisite for the adoption of a sanction is the commission of an internationally wrongful act. Among the hypotheses legitimizing the action of the Council under Chapter VII undoubtedly aggression constitutes an international wrongful act, but the other two? Rather they seem to cover situations of tension or conflict which do not necessarily amount to the violation of an international norm and not necessarily are attributable to international subjects. For example, in the case of the Somali conflict during the nineties, in the situation in which the Somali State was collapsing, it was not possible to identify any sovereign subject which could be held responsible of an internationally wrongful act and which could be, as such, the legitimate addressee of sanctions. In such cases measures adopted by the Council cannot be sanctions, because there are no international subjects which can be held responsible. Nor could it be affirmed that such situations confirm the theory of the international legal personality of individuals, who would become direct addresses of the sanctions by the Council. As such, sanctions consist of a reaction to a tort, in respect to which they must be proportionate, in their last purpose, they must be just, fair; further, sanctions must have a deterring effect and represent a sort of reparation for the victims injured by the illegal act; last but not least, sanctions shall have the purpose to induce the author of the illegal act to change its/her/his behaviour, they are, so to say, open to the future and take into account the concrete possibility to reintegrate the author of the wrongful act into the social community. But the measures not involving the use of force adopted by the Security Council are really far from possess only few among such features. Referring again to the case of Somalia, the Security Council sent a peace-keeping mission (UNOSOM) in order to try to appease the civil conflict and deliver humanitarian aid: the purpose of such measures does not resemble at all to «sanctions». Secondly, according to the Charter of the United Nations, the measures adopted by the Council must aim at maintaining or restoring international peace and security. These measures must be adopted in compliance with general international law and the letter of the Charter (see Articles 1, 2 and 24§2), but they are not aimed at restoring the infringed legal order. Nevertheless, the extension of the purpose of the measures adopted by the Council could however be welcomed in a legal order such as international law, if only the Council were the right body to ascertain the law and to sanction the wrongful acts. But the Council, a political body, hailed by many scholars as a world government *in nuce*, is not in itself suitable for performing the functions of an international judge[13]. The proof of such inadequacy of the Council to assume jurisdictional tasks lies in the selectivity with which it operates on the international scene. In some cases it adopts decisions (as it did in the Libyan affair in 2011), in others – even analogous to those in which it takes action – it remains inactive (think of the Syrian issue, so far not touched by measures adopted by the Council). The selectivity, the choice to act on purely political grounds and not motivated by the necessary consequentiality between violation and sanction, produces just the opposite of justice: in some cases certain States are targeted by the measures of the Council, in others they are not.

Therefore, not only the measures of the Council are not «sanctions», but it is also not appropriate for them to develop a function of this kind, due to the inability of a political body to guarantee law and justice, although, on the basis of express provisions of the Charter of the United Nations, it must itself act in a manner consistent with law (and certainly not as *legibus solutus*) and justice (see Article 1§1 of the Charter)[14].

---

[13] See very clearly on this point Gaetano Arangio-Ruiz, «The "Dual State", International Law and the UN: a Reply to Charles Leben», in Gaetano Arangio-Ruiz, Francesco Salerno, Cristiana Fioravanti, *Studi giuridici in ricordo di Giovanni Battaglini*, Jovene, Napoli 2013, pp. 1-42.

[14] According to Article 1§1, the main purposes of the United Nations are «[t]o maintain international peace and security, and to that end: to take effective collective measures for the prevention and removal of threats to the peace, and for the suppression of acts of aggression or other breaches of the peace, and to bring about by peaceful means, and in conformity with the principles of *justice* and international law, adjustment or settlement of international disputes or situations which might lead to a breach of the peace» (emphasis added).

5. (continued): The exceptions to the prohibition of the use of armed force: peace-keeping missions and their consensual foundation

In the previous paragraph, the description of the collective security system came to a halt after dealing with Article 42 of the Charter. Articles 43 ff., envisaging the creation of armies of the Security Council, in fact were never implemented, because the States never stipulated the agreements through which military contingents would be made available to the Council. Without resting on the conclusion, which could be drawn from this fact, of a never dormant distrust, on the part of the States, of the Council (thus further confirming the imprudence of those doctrinal visions favourable to expand its competences), here peace missions, bearing the blue helmet as a symbol of the United Nations, shall nevertheless be mentioned. Such military bodies do not constitute the implementation of Articles 43 ff. of the Charter, but they represent a sort of muted implementation of its original plot. They are set up to carry out *ad hoc* missions, created from time to time and sent in situations in which the sovereign subject is not adequately or is no longer able to maintain public order in its domestic jurisdiction or to perform typical state functions. The soldiers serving in peace-keeping forces are equipped only with light defence equipment, what confirms the non-aggressive nature of these missions, aimed at bringing back or maintaining (or «building», according to their mandate) peace in the interested areas. The conclusion for their non-aggressive character, although military, can be confirmed reflecting that, especially in recent years, their activity has been complemented and accompanied with those of organizations, including non-governmental organizations, aimed at monitoring and respecting human rights[15]. In general, peace-keeping missions are arranged through a resolution of the Security Council and their direction is entrusted to the Secretary-General, but such resolutions do not amount to authoritative intervention measures, since in the vast majority of cases (except for the hypothesis of the mission UNOSOM sent in the nineties to Somalia and for UNMIK, the mission created for Kosovo) these missions are based on the consent of the sovereign subject hosting them.

---

[15] See on this point Antonio Marchesi, *La protezione internazionale dei diritti umani. Nazioni Unite e organizzazioni regionali*, Franco Angeli, Milano 2011, p. 153 ff.

Due to the fact of joining the use of military means (an element regulated in Chapter VII of the Charter) and that of consensus (a key element of the competences referred to in Chapter VI), it was not without irony that some scholars intended to find the foundation of these missions in a «Chapter VI and ½ of the Charter», unwritten but consolidated by a practice of several decades.

As mentioned, the mandate of peace missions is determined *ad hoc*. It is possible to trace a historical evolution in the content of this mandate, testifying, over the time, how a broadening of the activities of these missions has been welcomed. Until the end of the Cold War, it peace-keeping operations essentially carried out activities inherent in the executive power (police activity). Subsequently, the adoption in 1992 of a document by UN Secretary General Boutros Ghali, «An Agenda for Peace», represented a turning point in the matter, since a connection was expressly made between maintenance of peace and protection of human rights: maintaining peace is a tool to protect human rights and, mutually, protecting human rights is a tool to maintain peace. Thanks to the connection between these two issues, which until then had been considered as two separate UN competences, the mandate of the peace-keeping missions has been extended to include the restructuring of internal institutions, the monitoring of respect for human rights, the organization of free democratic elections. In these cases, depending on the complexity of the mandate, in the present times we can record peace-enforcement or (when the intervention is more intense) peace-building missions.

6. (continued): The exceptions to the prohibition of the use of armed force: individual and collective self-defence and the resolutions of the Security Council authorizing the use of armed force

If these – just outlined and with the limits seen – are the only possibilities of using armed force in accordance with the Charter with the involvement of United Nations organs, for States as individual subjects, outside of the decision-making processes agreed under Chapter VII, the unilateral use of armed force remains fundamentally prohibited.

The only exception to this prohibition admitted by international law for the State acting unilaterally as an independent subject is self-defence, i.e. the action necessary – and insofar as it is necessary – to repel an armed attack already launched. Despite various attempts to expand the limits to which self-defence is subject, or to widen the types of unilateral armed measures considered admissible, the consolidation of further exceptions to the prohibition of the use of force does not seem to be legitimate. In particular, neither armed reprisals nor humanitarian intervention in situations of armed conflict outside the limits of self-defence can be considered admissible. Rather, above all in the case of reprisals, as finely argued[16] with the support of the judgment of the International Court of Justice on the case *Military and Paramilitary Activities in and Against Nicaragua*, the attempt to justify invoking self-defence cases of real armed retaliation (for example the armed measures adopted by the United States in Afghanistan shortly after the attack on the Twin Towers) paradoxically has the effect not of expanding the hypotheses in which the use of armed force is lawful, but on the contrary of strengthening the obligation contained in art. 2§4.

More problematic, on the other hand, is the case of armed measures adopted on the initiative of the United Nations Member States in implementation of UN Security Council resolutions. It shall be recalled, however, that such resolutions escape the limits of the Charter.

---

[16] Tullio Treves, *Diritto internazionale. Problemi fondamentali*, Giuffrè, Milano 2005, pp. 232-233.

As mentioned, the failure to stipulate the agreements referred to in Articles 43 ff. of the Charter has made it impossible to implement an effectively functioning collective security system. Part of the doctrine[17] tends to consider the failure to implement this part of the Charter as an example of abrogation by custom with a content contrary to the provisions of the treaty, what determines the extinction of the corresponding norms. Indeed, if we consider the failure to implement this part of the Charter as a form of a new customary rule adopted by subsequent practice, we could easily reach the conclusion that this phenomenon of obsolescence, while at the same time progressively affirming the peremptory nature of the prohibition to resort to armed force, has removed from the Security Council itself the competence to adopt armed measures. The same authors take this possibility into consideration, but then conclude – not without contradictions – rather for the negative solution[18]. But before addressing the question of whether the peremptory nature of the prohibition of the use of armed force should be considered as an insurmountable legal limit even for the armed operations promoted by the Council, it is necessary to examine briefly the practice of the organ to that account after the end of the Cold War.

A few months after the fall of the Berlin Wall, the Soviet Union was no longer in a political condition to veto many resolutions. So, the Council began a very intense activity which requires a complex evaluation in order to say whether, alongside the fall of the originally planned system (on which indeed there are few doubts), a new practice has been affirmed not only modifying the Charter, but also extending the possibilities of unilateral use of armed force. In other words: to the fall into disuse of the collective security system as a whole could correspond a consistent practice by the Security Council such as to allow in itself the formation of a new rule as regards the prohibition to use armed force. Already from putting the question in these terms, in my opinion we can see how the attempt to claim that «by now» a modification of the Charter (which, for its very delicate object was established with the 1945 Conference drafting precise, punctual regulations, certain as they are written, analytically discussed and object of

---

[17] See for instance Benedetto Conforti, Carlo Focarelli, *Le Nazioni Unite, op. cit.*, p. 278.
[18] Benedetto Conforti, Carlo Focarelli, *Le Nazioni Unite, op. cit.*, p. 266.

various hermeneutical battles), has been produced through a nebulous, inconstant, highly politicized practice, means to move on a very slippery ground. But we shall proceed step by step.

Certain is that, after so many years of inaction, starting from the end of the Cold War, the Council initiated a practice – in matters of Chapter VI but above all of Chapter VII – not in conformity with the letter of the Charter. The hyperactivity of the Council began in August 1990 following the attack by Iraq against Kuwait, when the organ began to adopt a resolution after another with the purpose to induce Iraq to withdraw its troops from Kuwaiti territory, first imposing measures not involving the use of armed force and then adopting the Resolution 678 (1990) with which, outside the limits of Chapter VII, it authorized the Member States to adopt « all necessary means», therefore also armed measures, if within a certain period Iraq did not withdraw from Kuwait. Some scholars, instead of stigmatizing this unorthodox way of acting by the Council, hastened to find props to justify what would later become the «authorizations to use armed force by the Council».

Pursuant to the Charter, the content of the measures implying the use of armed force referred to in Article 42 should first of all be punctually decided by the Council which should indicate the type of measures, similarly to what happens when, by deciding on an embargo, certain categories of assets are indicated, while other are excluded from the embargo measure. For example, Security Council 661 (1990) with which the embargo against Iraq was established (cf. text reproduced in the Appendix) provides to nos. 3 and 4 the blocking of all commercial traffic, including an arms embargo, as well as the freezing of funds owned by Iraqi citizens abroad, while exempting certain categories of assets considered essential for the survival of the civilian population. In other words, it does not say to states: «take all the necessary measures against Iraq», since such a delegation would represent just the opposite of a centralized crisis management. Therefore, to return to the issues of authorization for the use of armed force, the formula «all necessary measures» is first of all too vague and undetermined, and the measures so vaguely indicated cannot *per se* be evaluated under the point of view of their purpose, i.e., the maintenance or restoration of the peace which represents a specific limit as regards any action by the Council.

Secondly and above all, such armed measures could not be left to the arbitrariness of the States, but should be directed and managed by the Council itself through the never established Military Staff Committee. The authorization given to Member States to use «all the necessary measures», adopting the vague formulation in the sense said above, does not correspond to the letter of the Charter, since the latter does not envisage in any of its provisions such possibility as an alternative to the creation of the collective security system. In none of its Articles it is written that the Council will authorize the Member States to use in full discretion any kind of armed measure, thus reviving the faculty of the use of armed force unilaterally. Indeed, it is precisely this possibility of reviving the use of armed force *uti singuli* what the founding States of the United Nations, mindful of the disaster of two World Wars, had tried to avoid, and such an attempt was somehow successful – paradoxically, given the failure of the collective security system – even with the balances imposed during the entire Cold War.

Faced with the novelty represented by the lacking of the Soviet veto, what allowed the Council to function after decades of almost complete inactivity, more than one argument was proposed by the doctrine to support the legitimacy of Resolution 678 (1990) authorising «to use all necessary means». The first (in time) and perhaps the most recognized of these arguments is the one interpreting such authorization as a measure of collective self-defence[19]. By invoking the «inherent right of collective self-defence» (see the text of Article 51 of the Charter of the United Nations) as an institution of general international law, which actually could never be compressed or reduced by any international agreement – as an institution rooted in the very essence of law international and perhaps of law in general –, such doctrine made an attempt to find a justification based on one of the cornerstones of international law. But if we consider the whole question closer, such attempt to justification vacillates when analyzed in the light of the legal requirements established by international law for resorting to self-defence.

---

[19] In Italy such view was supported by Giorgio Gaja, «Il Consiglio di Sicurezza di fronte all'occupazione del Kuwait: il significato di una autorizzazione», in *Rivista di diritto internazionale,* 1990, pp. 696-697.

Some further justifications proposed shall be considered.

A) Collective self-defence. First of all, the action in self-defence must be the *ultima ratio* after having tried all possible alternative ways. In fact, before authorizing the adoption of «all necessary means» through Resolution 678 (1990), the Security Council not only had repeatedly urged Iraq to withdraw its troops from Kuwait, but had also taken this decision after a series of measures not involving the use of armed force have proved to be ineffective. However, chronicling back those months of great tension, the general impression is that on that occasion the Council was rather in a hurry to arrange the adoption of armed measures, as if it were driven by a sort of anxiety to function – finally, after so many years of paralysis due to the Cold War. But even if we want to consider the content of the Resolution 678 as the ultimate means after a series of unsuccessful attempts to solve the question pacifically, the problem of proportionality remains as an indispensable requirement of the measure adopted in self-defence. The requirement of proportionality is rooted in law as a phenomenon: as already mentioned, since the emergence of modern international society, proportionality has been a criterion for assessing the legitimacy of the use of armed force, both defensively and for sanctioning purposes. Proportionality is a correspondence between action and reaction, it is a characterizing element of the legal relationship as such, that is, as what establishes a relationship between two subjects permeated by law. If we reflect further, it is precisely this requirement what allows us to consider law as a system, that is, as a framework of correspondences, more or less complex, which can be found at the microscopic level at the heart of the legal relationship as the first cell of this system. Individual self-defence is considered lawful in international law when it takes the form of deploying the force necessary to repel the occurring armed attack. First of all it is the attacked State the subject which has the right to defend itself. In the event considered, the Kuwaiti government had instead sheltered in the United States and no longer had control of its military means in order to repel the Iraqi invasion. So at this point the question of «collective self-defence» takes over, that is, the possibility of an intervention conducted by several subjects (who, however, have not suffered any aggression) acting for defensive purposes for the benefit of a subject which, alone, cannot defend itself. But are we certain that the so called Gulf War, interpreted as a legitimate measure of collective self-defence, with its operations with high-sounding names «Desert Storm» and the like, conducted by military powers such as those of the United States, Great Britain, France, etc. allied for the occasion, respected the requirement of proportionality? The methods of conducting those military operations which cost the lives of many civilians leave serious doubts in this regard.

But even if we want to ignore – but only for the moment – these effects on the civilian population, although at first glance it is obvious («inherent») to admit this juridical institution, a more careful reflection shows that the collective self-defence in itself is a very problematic figure, precisely from the point of view of proportionality: in fact there are more States intervening to protect (in some cases to free) one State attacked by another: it consists *per se* in the concerted action of many against one. I would be tempted to say that, compared with individual self-defence, collective self-defence operates rather as a deterrent, a function much more proper to a sanction and which does not fit the strictly defensive purpose of this institution. To draw a difference between sanctions and self-defence, it is precisely the requirement of proportionality what *prima facie* must be evaluated differently. In the case of the sanction it is not excluded to expect an afflictive feature (as it is required for example in the case of satisfaction or punitive damages), what instead remains extraneous to the purely defensive function of self-defence as an action strictly commensurate with the attack to be rejected. Given that in current international law the use of armed force for sanctioning purposes is no longer permitted, collective self-defence should have become unlawful at least for its sanctioning (afflictive) part. But – one could argue – in a legal order as peculiar (as «primitive») as international law, one could not exclude that collective (unlike individual) self-defence, in addition to the defensive purpose, also presents an afflictive purpose emerging from the same possibility that more States arm themselves against a only aggressor state. But the fact is that the practice in the matter of collective self-defence does not make it possible to consider a similar afflictive character of collective self-defence as legitimate, since this practice is not free from contradictions

35

or criticisms. Indeed, collective self-defence is not resorted to significantly often, in a constant, reliable manner, so that it could reasonably be concluded that it assumed, along the centuries, a deterrent purpose and ultimately sanctioning function. On the contrary, apart the patent case of Iraqi aggression against Kuwait followed by the military action authorized by UN Security Council, indubitable, effective cases of collective self-defence with which to make a comparison are really few. Furthermore, even if some armed intervention has been traced back to the figure of collective self-defence (for instance the US intervention in Vietnam or the Korean war), many criticisms are raised in these cases and many questions of conformity with the UN Charter on which here it is not possible to dwell remain unanswered.

But even if we wanted to admit this ultimate purpose, in essence a sanctioning function, of collective self-defence, then we should complain about the failure to adopt it in similar hypotheses: one could think of the case of the long-standing Israeli-Palestinian conflict; more recently the cases of Syrian and Ukrainian crises. In such cases no action in collective self-defence has been adopted; so that one could conclude that in such situations such an action did not seem an adequate measure for the UN Member States. It does not therefore seem that collective self-defence has acquired through practice a sanctioning function; as a consequence, the measure adopted for this purpose must be kept strictly within the limits of proportionality and the function of rejecting the armed attack.

B) Implied powers. Going back to the legitimacy of Security Council resolutions authorizing the use of «all necessary means», we shall recall that in addition to collective self-defence, some scholars have invoked the theory of implied powers, which among other things has served for argumentative purposes to give foundation not only to authorizations for the use of armed force but also to other activities of the Council not included in the letter of the Charter and also dating back to the nineties, such as the establishment of two *ad hoc* tribunals to adjudicate individual crimes committed in the former Yugoslavia and in Rwanda. The theory of implied powers is invoked to extend the powers of a common body beyond what is laid down in its founding act on the basis of the consideration that the body must implicitly be endowed with all those powers necessary to achieve the purposes of its function. According to this doctrine, in order to maintain international peace and security, the Security Council could therefore have additional powers or powers beyond those established in the Charter. Now, if the theory of implied powers meets, after all, little resistance within organizations aimed at building an integration between States (a prime example being that of the European Union), in a matter so important like the maintenance of international peace and security within an Organization based on the principle of sovereign equality and not aiming at political nor legal integration, it is certainly more difficult to leave room for such a vague extension of the competences of a highly politicized body such as the United Nations Security Council. Applying the theory of implied powers in the light of a general purpose as the «maintenance of international peace and security», would leave completely undetermined the competences of the organ and it would make the application of the law very uncertain. Here, too, the problem is heightened by the selective nature of the Council's activity. The point is that in some cases the Council acts, in others it remains completely inert, thus reinforcing the impression of not contributing to the affirmation neither of international law nor of justice in crisis management. According to Article 1 of the Charter, end of the Organization (and, according to the art. 24§2, specific purpose which must inspire the action of the Security Council), in fact, it is not only the maintenance of international peace and security, but also «to achieve by peaceful means, and *in accordance with the principles of justice and international law*, the settlement or resolution of disputes or international situations that could lead to a violation of peace» (emphasis added). The purpose of maintaining peace must therefore be counterbalanced with that one of achieving respect for international law and justice as instruments able to promote peace and prevent a possible worsening of the situation. The selective orientation characterizing the action of the Council in recent years certainly contravenes this principle and in my opinion does not permit to invoke the theory of implied powers in order to legitimize very questionable choices, whose final outcome is in substance to expand the possibilities of use of armed force outside the very strict limits set by art. 2§4 and from Chapter VII.

C) Modification of the Charter by subsequent practice. Another thesis which seeks a justification for this problematic Council practice is, as already mentioned, that one which invokes the formation of a new practice modifying the letter of the Charter. Given the flexibility of rank between custom and agreement in international law, the unwritten custom can be modified by the written agreement and the latter, in turn, can be modified by a practice of application differing from what was originally intended in the treaty. A subsequent practice based on the consent by the States would therefore in principle be appropriate to modify the letter of the Charter in the sense that States, *de facto*, through their own behaviour, would have agreed to widen the limits of action of the Council. Now, actually, if we take the time to read the verbatim records of the meetings at the Council concerning those problematic decisions concerning the authorization to use «all necessary means», we can see that, within the Council itself, some Member States, although relegated to a minority, did not at all agree with the initiatives to authorize the use of armed force promoted by the organ. Since only 15 States sit in the Council, it is difficult to argue that this organ embodies the will of the UN Member States and, what is more, therefore its activities express the will of all Member States to accept those modifications to the Charter that have occurred by way of practice. In a very recent case, that of Resolution 2161 of 15 August 2014, the Security Council «calls upon» the adoption of all the measures as necessary and appropriate against the groups of terrorists currently operating in Iraq[20]. It is on the basis of this «recommendation» that the United States paved the way to the launch of a series of bombings of Iraqi territory to put an end to the serious facts perpetrated by ISIL members. Although Resolution 2161 was adopted unanimously, on the basis of a full consensus of the international community regarding the legitimacy of armed measures adopted, in reality if we read the position statements of the States made a few weeks

---

[20] «The Security Council [...]6. Reiterates its call upon all States to take all measures as may be necessary and appropriate and in accordance with their obligations under international law to counter incitement of terrorist acts motivated by extremism and intolerance perpetrated by individuals or entities associated with ISIL, ANF and Al-Qaida and to prevent the subversion of educational, cultural, and religious institutions by terrorists and their supporters».

earlier at the General Assembly[21], we note several voices expressly opposed to the adoption of armed measures, such as the particularly clear Senegal, sharing the view that dialogue and tolerance promoting mutual respect between all cultures, beliefs and religions should be developed. To this opinion other similar were added, most of all those emphasizing, on the one hand, how the use of force is not the proper means in order to eradicate terrorism (opinion shared by the Egyptian, Kyrgyz, Australian, Brazilian, Malay delegates), and, on the other hand, the fight against terrorism cannot renounce the adoption of measures which in any case respect human rights and the lives of civilians innocents, as well as the principle of the rule of law (point emphasized by the delegates of Mexico, Cameroon, Costa Rica, Algeria, Spain, Russia, Norway, France, Colombia, Morocco, Republic of Korea, Argentina, Qatar, European Union and again Brazil). As can be seen from the large number of these positions, it is in my opinion an alteration of reality to affirm that the international community «by now» agrees with the use of armed force only because the Security Council decides it.

A further difficulty to legitimize the Council's practice of authorizing the use of armed force is represented by the fact that the prohibition of the use of armed force is binding, and therefore if the consent of a group of States in a given political conjuncture it is not able to represent that of all the Member States, when the modifying of an ordinary agreement is at stake, even less it is able to modify a peremptory norm embodying and protecting interests of the entire international community as a whole, thus also involving all the international subjects which are not parties to the United Nations.

How can we assess this disturbing Council practice? In my opinion it can only – and not without discomfort – be concluded that in certain situations the Council has succeeded in acting – overriding its own statutory limits – simply by taking advantage of the political contingency, that is to say, the weakness of some permanent Members which in other cases can paralyze the organ completely. The political contingency, as such, is not able to constitute a reliable point of reference to verify the occurrence of a modification of a written norm. Rather, the reality is that there are no effective control

---

[21] See General Assembly, Doc. 11522 of 12 June 2014.

mechanisms to sanction any unlawful conduct by the Security Council. But it is the same sporadic nature of its initiatives that must warn against the affirmation of the modification of the Charter by custom.

D) Use of regional arrangements. A final argument in support of the legitimacy of the authorizations to use armed force adopted by the Council refers to the «regional arrangements» mentioned in Chapter VIII of the Charter[22]. Especially Article 53 would serve to this end, because it provides that the Council may possibly use regional arrangements or bodies for the implementation of its own coercive measures and that in any case such agreements or regional bodies cannot act without the authorization of the Security Council. The word «authorization» in this Article was the pretext to deduce a generic as well as elusive power of the Council to authorize anything. This rule was used arguing in this way: the allied forces involved in the Gulf War in 1991 and in the other actions in which the use of force was authorized constitute regional arrangements (given that for the most part they were agreements between political powers neighbours, i.e. States of the former Western bloc). Therefore, if the States bound by these agreements cannot act without the authorization of the Council, then the authorization of the Council removes the obstacle to joint armed action conducted in accordance with such agreements or regional bodies.

Indeed, Article 53 seems to have been envisaged for other situations. First of all, according to the Charter, it is the Council which must have decided on the measures to be taken, and must resort to agreements or regional bodies for the concrete implementation of such measures as they have already been specifically decided by the Council: the indication of «all measures necessary» really seems a too broad formula to avoid the abuses that the delegation to unilateral action of several States without the specific control of the Council inevitably brings with it. Furthermore, if I read correctly the temporal structure of the situation giving rise to the possibility to invoke Article 53, *first*, agreements or regional bodies able to operate in certain situations (compatibly with the Charter of the United Nations, according to the art. 103 of the latter, therefore never

---

[22] See Benedetto Conforti, Carlo Focarelli, *Le Nazioni Unite, op. cit.*, p. 345 ff.

in order to use armed force outside the limits of the Charter, but – if ever – in order to favour the peaceful settlement of disputes, as stated in the same Article 52§§ 2 and 3 of the Charter) are established, and eventually the Council can use them for the concrete implementation of coercive measures which it has precisely decided. In other words, there is a procedural scan which is not respected in the case of authorizations to use force decided by the Council: in fact, such authorizations do not give permission to already existing regional arrangements to concretely adopt the measures which in principle the Council should manage, but have the effect of authorizing the formation of *ad hoc* agreements – subsequent to the Council's decision – to use armed force without making, on their own, any effort to find a peaceful solution as they should under Article. 52§3. In other words, it seems to me that such a ploy to invoke Article 53 in order to justify the authorizations to use «all necessary means», betrays the letter of the Charter.

Among other things, given that since the birth of the United Nations, in the meantime the prohibition of the use of armed force has assumed the rank of a peremptory norm, that is to say, among other things, a norm which cannot be derogated even by consensus, these *ad hoc* agreements which would have arisen later, as agreements with which an armed action is carried out (outside the limits of the aforementioned self-defence), shall be null and void by contrast with *jus cogens*[23]. It is unlikely to claim that the resolution of an organ like the Security Council, composed of a handful of States is sufficient to flex the rigid nature of a peremptory rule such as the prohibition of the use of armed force, the first on the list of examples of fundamental norms according to Draft Article 19 proposed by Roberto Ago as he was *Special Rapporteur* on State Responsibility at the International Law Commission.

The United Nations themselves, as a subject of international law, are bound to respect this peremptory rule, and even from this point of view, it should be asked (as we will try to do in the last paragraph) whether the emergence of the peremptory norms does not require a rethinking of the competences of the UN as an international subject in order to render the guarantees for a peaceful coexistence of international subjects more effective.

---

[23] See Articles 53 and 64 of Vienna Convention on the law of treaties.

7. (continues): The exceptions to the prohibition of the use of armed force: some considerations on humanitarian intervention

Given what has been said so far, if the authorizations for the use of armed force reveal so many problems of compatibility with the Charter, even more problematic is the practice of *ex post facto* authorization inaugurated with the Security Council Resolution 1244 (1999) a few months after the attack launched by NATO in the territory of the former Yugoslavia for «humanitarian» purposes, that is to face the emergency represented by the very serious violations of human rights perpetrated in that area. The NATO operation was conducted without the prior authorization of the United Nations Security Council, which, according to some authors, nevertheless, precisely with Resolution 1244 would have remedied this original lack of legitimacy. Now, in my opinion, if there can be so many doubts about the practice of prior authorization to use the armed force by the Council, even more serious one may arise only to imagine a subsequent authorization with the effect of amnesty of an armed action which presents in itself an incurable contradiction between its purpose and its material way to operate: that is to say, protecting the violation of human rights through the use of armed force, that is what in itself produces a violation of fundamental human rights (right to life, to physical integrity and safety, to the freedom of movement, to property and so on).

It should be noted that on the one hand, the armed intervention by NATO in 1999 during the Kosovo crisis raised a great deal of criticism and doubts about its legitimacy among the scholars, who highlighted how States which took part in it had issued contradictory statements regarding this affair, denoting a very uncertain legal basis[24]. On the other hand, the same opinions in favour of the intervention justified it only as an exceptional situation (the extraordinary grave violation of human rights) requiring the adoption of *extra ordinem* measures. I have already discussed elsewhere the general danger that lurks in the attempts to open the gates represented by the state of exception in law, allow me to refer the reader to the words already spent in that place, without repeating myself[25]. Here, recalling NATO intervention in 1999 – but the same doubts could be cast on other armed interventions justified (at least in part) on a

---

[24] Tullio Treves, *Diritto internazionale, op. cit.*, pp. 469-470.
[25] See Giuliana Scotto, *Riflessioni su stato di eccezione, diritto internazionale e sovranità*, Roma, Aracne, 2008.

humanitarian basis, as in the case of the intervention in Iraq in 2003 and the one in Libya in 2011 – is useful to illustrate how the matter is far from consolidating certain criteria that precisely defines the preconditions, the type of measures allowed, the peremptory limits to which the armed intervention – if ever admissible – must submit.

What is certain, is that a distinction must be drawn between humanitarian intervention in situations caused by natural disasters and that in situations produced by armed conflicts. For the first type of intervention not only the consent of the State affected by the natural catastrophe does seem necessary – as evidenced for example by the case of Japan, which denied entry to humanitarian operations following the earthquake and subsequent tsunami in 2011. But even the type of measures which are taken in such circumstances seem to be really geared towards bringing relief to the population hit by the disaster: the use of military means in an emergency situation caused by a natural disaster should aim not at using armed force to put an end to human activities (and lives), but for example at delivering material aid (medical stuff, food, water), ensuring care of the wounded, reconstruction of infrastructures etc. A similar type of humanitarian intervention would seem in principle admissible; especially the consent by the target State removes the obstacles to the intrusion in a foreign territory by armed means (unless, of course, the military operations do not conceal real intentions against the territorial integrity and political independence of an international entity, in the terms of the prohibition referred to in Article 2§4 of the Charter).

In the case, instead, of an external intervention in case of armed conflict in progress within a State or in the territory of several States, the use of armed force for humanitarian purposes would serve in good part to dissuade people who commit serious crimes from continuing to perpetrate their brutalities. But the problem is that this would not be a work of convincing, so to speak, with good things, through reasonableness, through examples showing the sacredness of personal integrity and the inestimable value of human existence. Quite the opposite, in such cases humanitarian intervention is the use of means which, by bombing, razing cities, sometimes even by affecting the civilian population, imply that human life in certain cases – although exceptional – can be legitimately destroyed. On this respect, I can only try to shed light on this point, which seems to me an irreconcilable contradiction.

However, it is perhaps not without significance even in the case of the recent NATO summit called at the beginning of September 2014 to decide, among other things, on the fate of the affair between Russia and Ukraine, despite the prospect of the possible creation of a rapid force of reaction (which I would consider illegitimate) composed of five thousand soldiers, in fact, apparently this force will not be used since a solid truce seems to have begun between the two States involved.

8. Jus cogens *and the obligation to respect it also by the United Nations as a subject of general international law*

At this point, a step forward seems inevitable, opening up to the possibilities of development of international law inherent in the notion of *jus cogens.*

Hopefully, I have shown with sufficient clarity how the attempts to justify the Security Council's practice reveal themselves inadequate before the proving ground of the necessary consequence to interpret and apply the law. In many cases the practice of the Security Council has produced the effect of inducing States to use armed force, mostly through the authorization to use «all the necessary means». But, as pointed out many times, in contemporary international law, the use of armed force is now illegal and this illegality cannot be easily removed (i.e. by mutual consent), because the norm envisaging it is a peremptory rule. It was the same practice of the States and of the organs of the United Nations to reach such goal, and not only for the notion of peremptory rule was codified thanks to the Vienna Convention on the law of treaties and then to Ago's Draft Article on international crimes of States.

Even a myriad of other facts has given this line of development substance and breadth on a global level. First of all, today we are faced with a consistent number of both bilateral obligations (many of which entered into force during the Cold War) and multilateral disarmament obligations, which have banned the use of certain types of weapons: like the Treaty on the Non-Proliferation of Nuclear Weapons of 1968; the Convention on Biological Weapons of 1972; the 1987 Intermediate-Range Nuclear

Force Treaty; the 1990 Treaty on Conventional Armed Forces in Europe; the Convention on the Prohibition of Chemical Weapons of 1993; the Convention on the Prohibition of the Use, Stockpiling, Production and Transfer of Anti-Personnel Mines and on their Destruction in 1997; the Convention on cluster munitions of 2008). These disarmament obligations constitute an important practical reinforcement of the prohibition of the use of armed force as a peremptory norm, since they increasingly limit the possibility to use armed means, better illuminating the perspective which considers peace and respect for life human as ultimate goals which cannot be renounced.

The same failure to implement the collective security system (Articles 43 ff. of the United Nations Charter) during all these years can be read not as the mere effect of the Cold War[26], but rather as a confirmation of the firm will of the Member States not to equip the Council with military means, even if in order to employ them in the terms of the Charter. If one absolutely wants to derive from this practice the evidence of an agreement to modify the Charter, this is, unequivocally in the sense of longer considering the Council as an organ capable of adequately managing crises, and that is why it has not been provided with the material means to manage crisis as States had originally established by adhering to the Charter. Therefore, applying to the case of the United Nations Article 64 of the 1969 Vienna Convention on the Law of Treaties (regulating the case of *jus cogens superveniens*), one can come to the conclusion that this part of the Charter in which mechanisms for the adoption of armed measures other than individual self-defence shall be considered as null and void for they are contrary to a peremptory norm, that is the one prohibiting the use of armed force. This contrariety to a peremptory norm determines the impossibility of a revival of the possibility to resort to force due to practice of few States. For decades – and the current situation is not different from this point of view – therefore States preferred not to provide the Council with concrete opportunities to function as it should have done, i.e. using armed force. At the same time, it must be borne in mind that in parallel States have affirmed, consolidated, reiterated in many situations and occasions the full validity of the

---

[26] As proposed for instance by Gaetano Arangio-Ruiz, «The "Dual State", International Law and the UN: a Reply to Charles Leben», *op. cit.*, p. 32.

prohibition of the use of armed force, welcoming the possibility of considering it as a peremptory norm, as confirmed several times also by international courts including the International Court of Justice.

The rules of *jus cogens* are peremptory towards all the subjects of the international community, that is to say also for the United Nations and the bodies through which they act. It is time to say that the use of armed force is completely banned and that the Security Council not only cannot manage international crises by force because States have decided not to provide them with military forces for this purpose, but nor can it authorize this use of force, because the practice of the States has been oriented to consider this prohibition as a peremptory rule, and also the United Nations (through all their organs), as a subject of international law they are bound to respect it[27]. The doctrine which also captures the clarity and consistency of this conclusion[28] then ends up admitting the use of armed force through the authorization of the Security Council, and this for two essential reasons. On the one hand, this doctrine maintains that peremptory rules would not have «clear content». But it is evident that this is a specious argument, because on the four examples of mandatory rules proposed in the Draft Article 19 proposed by Ago there are no obscure points as regards the content of the rules, especially the one concerning the prohibition of resorting to armed force.

On the other hand, this doctrinal position notes an inextricable contradiction between two types of peremptory rules, namely the prohibition of the use of force on the one hand, and the need to safeguard (by armed force) human rights on the other side. But here, too, the captiousness of this conclusion appears in all its evidence: as mentioned above, the contradiction lies in protecting human rights with bombs, with the use of weapons, with the possibility to make mistakes by hitting targets at the expense of the civilian population.

---

[27] That also international organizations are bound to international law is stressed also by Gaetano Arangio-Ruiz, «The "Dual State", International Law and the UN: a Reply to Charles Leben», *op. cit.*, p. 34.
[28] Benedetto Conforti, Carlo Focarelli, *Le Nazioni Unite*, *op. cit.*, p. 266.

As highlighted in *An Agenda for Peace*, the connection must be made not between human rights and use of force, but between human rights and peace. Peace is instrumental to the affirmation of rights, and respect for human rights is a tool to maintain peace. Only respect for the rights and life of human beings can safeguard peace and coexistence between States.

In short, it is time that the Security Council, as the body of an international entity, also respects the prohibition of the use of armed force as a norm of *jus cogens*.

Appendix:

Definition of Aggression, United Nations General Assembly Resolution 3314 (XXIX)[29].

The General Assembly,

Having considered the report of the Special Committee on the Question of Defining Aggression, established pursuant to its resolution 2330(XXII) of 18 December 1967, covering the work of its seventh session held from 11 March to 12 April 1974, including the draft Definition of Aggression adopted by the Special Committee by consensus and recommended for adoption by the General Assembly,

Deeply, convinced that the adoption of the Definition of Aggression would contribute to the strengthening of international peace and security,

1. Approves the Definition of Aggression, the text of which is annexed to the present resolution;

2. Expresses its appreciation to the Special Committee on the Question of Defining Aggression for its work which resulted in the elaboration of the Definition of Aggression;

3. Calls upon all States to refrain from all acts of aggression and other uses of force contrary to the Charter of the United Nations and the Declaration on Principles of International Law concerning Friendly Relations and Cooperation among States in accordance with the Charter of the United Nations;

4. Calls the attention of the Security Council to the Definition of Aggression, as set out below, and recommends that it should, as appropriate, take account of that Definition as guidance in determination, in accordance with the Charter, the existence of an act of aggression.

2319th plenary meeting

14 December 1974

Annex – Definition of Aggression

The General Assembly,

Basing itself on the fact that one of the fundamental purposes of the United Nations is to maintain international peace and security and to take effective collective measures for the prevention and removal of threats to the peace, and for the suppression of acts of aggression or other breaches of the peace,

Recalling that the Security Council, in accordance with Article 39 of the Charter of the United Nations, shall determine the existence of any threat to the peace, breach of the peace or act of aggression and

---

[29] The text of the General Assembly Resolution can be free downloaded at the United Nations website: https://documents-dds-ny.un.org/doc/RESOLUTION/GEN/NR0/739/16/IMG/NR073916.pdf?OpenElement.

shall make recommendations, or decide what measures shall be taken in accordance with Articles 41 and 42, to maintain or restore international peace and security,

Recalling also the duty of States under the Charter to settle their international disputes by peaceful means in order not to endanger international peace, security and justice,

Bearing in mind that nothing in this Definition shall be interpreted as in any way affecting the scope of the provisions of the Charter with respect to the functions and powers of the organs of the United Nations,

Considering also that, since aggression is the most serious and dangerous form of the illegal use of force, being fraught, in the conditions created by the existence of all types of weapons of mass destruction, with the possible threat of a world conflict and all its catastrophic consequences, aggression should be defined at the present stage,

Reaffirming the duty of States not to use armed force to deprive peoples of their right to self-determination, freedom and independence, or to disrupt territorial Integrity,

Reaffirming also that the territory of a State shall not be violated by being the object, even temporarily, of military occupation or of other measures of force taken by another State in contravention of the Charter, and that it shall not be the object of acquisition by another State resulting from such measures or the threat thereof,

Reaffirming also the provisions of the Declaration on Principles of International Law concerning Friendly Relations and Cooperation among States in accordance with the Charter of the United Nations,

Convinced that the adoption of a definition of aggression ought to have the effect of deterring a potential aggressor, would simplify the determination of acts of aggression and the implementation of measures to suppress them and would also facilitate the protection of the rights and lawful interests of, and the rendering of assistance to, the victim,

Believing that, although the question whether an act of aggression has been committed must be considered in the light of all the circumstances of each particular case, it is nevertheless desirable to formulate basic principles as guidance for such determination,

Adopts the following Definition of Aggression:

Article I

Aggression is the use of armed force by a State against the sovereignty, territorial integrity or political independence of another State, or in any other manner inconsistent with the Charter of the United Nations, as set out in this Definition.

Explanatory note: In this Definition the term «State»:

(a) Is used without prejudice to questions of recognition or to whether a State is a member of the United Nations;

(b) Includes the concept of a «group of States» where appropriate.

Article 2

The First use of armed force by a State in contravention of the Charter shall constitute prima facie evidence of an act of aggression although the Security Council may, in conformity with the Charter, conclude that a determination that an act of aggression has been committed would not be justified in the light of other relevant circumstances, including the fact that the acts concerned or their consequences are not of sufficient gravity.

Article 3

Any of the following acts, regardless of a declaration of war, shall, subject to and in accordance with the provisions of Article 2, qualify as an act of aggression:

(a) The invasion or attack by the armed forces of a State of the territory of another State, or any military occupation, however temporary, resulting from such invasion or attack, or any annexation by the use of force of the territory of another State or part thereof,

(b) Bombardment by the armed forces of a State against the territory of another State or the use of any weapons by a State against the territory of another State;

(c) The blockade of the ports or coasts of a State by the armed forces of another State;

(d) An attack by the armed forces of a State on the land, sea or air forces, or marine and air fleets of another State;

(e) The use of armed forces of one State which are within the territory of another State with the agreement of the receiving State, in contravention of the conditions provided for in the agreement or any extension of their presence in such territory beyond the termination of the agreement;

(f) The action of a State in allowing its territory, which it has placed at the disposal of another State, to be used by that other State for perpetrating an act of aggression against a third State;

(g) The sending by or on behalf of a State of armed bands, groups, irregulars or mercenaries, which carry out acts of armed force against another State of such gravity as to amount to the acts listed above, or its substantial involvement therein.

Article 4

The acts enumerated above are not exhaustive and the Security Council may determine that other acts constitute aggression under the provisions of the Charter.

Article 5

1. No consideration of whatever nature, whether political, economic, military or otherwise, may serve as a justification for aggression.

2. A war of aggression is a crime against international peace. Aggression gives rise to international responsibility.

3. No territorial acquisition or special advantage resulting from aggression is or shall be recognized as lawful.

Article 6

Nothing in this Definition shall be construed as in any way enlarging or diminishing the scope of the Charter, including its provisions concerning cases in which the use of force is lawful.

Article 7

Nothing in this Definition, and in particular Article 3, could in any way prejudice the right to self-determination, freedom and independence, as derived from the Charter, of peoples forcibly deprived of that right and referred to in the Declaration on Principles of International Law concerning Friendly Relations and Cooperation among States in accordance with the Charter of the United Nations, particularly peoples under colonial and racist regimes or other forms of alien domination: nor the right of these peoples to struggle to that end and to seek and receive support, in accordance with the principles of the Charter and in conformity with the above-mentioned Declaration.

Article 8

In their interpretation and application the above provisions are interrelated and each provision should be construed in the context of the other provisions.

_____

Security Council Resolution 661 (1990) of 6 August 1990[30]

The Security Council,

Reaffirming its resolution 660 (1990) of 2 August 1990,

Deeply concerned that that resolution has not been implemented and that the invasion by Iraq of Kuwait continues, with further loss of human life and material destruction,

Determined to bring the invasion and occupation of Kuwait by Iraq to an end and to restore the sovereignty, independence and territorial integrity of Kuwait,

Noting that the legitimate Government of Kuwait has expressed its readiness to comply with resolution 660 (1990),

Mindful of its responsibilities under the Charter of the United Nations for the maintenance of international peace and security,

Affirming the inherent right of individual or collective self-defence, in response to the armed attack by Iraq against Kuwait, in accordance with Article 51 of the Charter,

_____

[30] The text of the Security Council Resolution No. 661 (1990) can be free downloaded at the United Nations website: https://documents-dds-ny.un.org/doc/RESOLUTION/GEN/NR0/575/11/IMG/NR057511.pdf?OpenElement.

Acting under Chapter VII of the Charter,

1. Determines that Iraq so far has failed to comply with paragraph 2 of resolution 660 (1990) and has usurped the authority of the legitimate Government of Kuwait;

2. Decides, as a consequence, to take the following measures to secure compliance ofIraq with paragraph 2 of resolution 660 (1990) and to restore the authority of the legitimate Government of Kuwait;

3. Decides that all States shall prevent:

(a) The import into their territories of all commodities and products originating in Iraq or Kuwait exported therefrom after the date of the present resolution;

(b) Any activities by their nationals or in their territories which would promote or are calculated to promote the export or trans-shipment of any commodities or products from Iraq or Kuwait; and any dealings by their nationals or their flag vessels or in their territories in any commodities or products originating in Iraq or Kuwait and exported therefrom after the date of the present resolution, including in particular any transfer of funds to Iraq or Kuwait for the purposes of such activities or dealings;

(c) The sale or supply by their nationals or from their territories or using their flag vessels of any commodities or products, including weapons or any other military equipment, whether or not originating in their territories but not including supplies intended strictly for medical purposes, and, in humanitarian circumstances, foodstuffs, to any person or body in Iraq or Kuwait or to any person or body for the purposes of any business carried on in or operated from Iraq or Kuwait, and any activities by their nationals or in their territories which promote or are calculated to promote such sale or supply of such commodities or products;

4. Decides that all States shall not make available to the Government of Iraq, or to any commercial, industrial or public utility undertaking in Iraq or Kuwait, any funds or any other financial or economic resources and shall prevent their nationals and any persons within their territories from removing from their territories or otherwise making available to that Government or to any such undertaking any such funds or resources and from remitting any other funds to persons or bodies within Iraq or Kuwait, except payments exclusively for strictly medical or humanitarian purposes and, in humanitarian circumstances, foodstuffs;

5. Calls upon all States, including States non-members of the United Nations, to act strictly in accordance with the provisions of the present resolution notwithstanding any contract entered into or licence granted before the date of the present resolution;

6. Decides to establish, in accordance with rule 28 of the provisional rules of procedure, a Committee of the Security Council consisting of all the members of the Council, to undertake the following tasks and to report on its work to the Council with its observations and recommendations:

(a) To examine the reports on the progress of the implementation of the present resolution which will be submitted by the Secretary-General;

(b) To seek from all States further information regarding the action taken by them concerning the effective implementation of the provisions laid down in the present resolution;

7. Calls upon all States to co-operate fully with the Committee in the fulfilment of its tasks, including supplying such information as may be sought by the Committee in pursuance of the present resolution;

8. Requests the Secretary-General to provide all necessary assistance to the Committee and to make the necessary arrangements in the Secretariat for that purpose;

9. Decides that, notwithstanding paragraphs 4 to 8 above, nothing in the present resolution shall prohibit assistance to the legitimate Government of Kuwait, and calls upon all States:

(a) To take appropriate measures to protect assets of the legitimate Government of Kuwait and its agencies;

(b) Not to recognize any regime set up by the occupying Power;

10. Requests the Secretary-General to report to the Security Council on the progress made in the implementation of the present resolution, the first report to be submitted within thirty days;

11. Decides to keep this item on its agenda and to continue its efforts to put an early end to the invasion by Iraq.